JV Non Fiction
j 792.02 L831i

Loh—Hagan, Virginia, author. Improv show
9001133666

Y0-EAH-747

DISCARDED
Mead Public Library

D.I.Y. MAKE IT HAPPEN

IMPROV SHOW

VIRGINIA LOH-HAGAN

45th Parallel Press

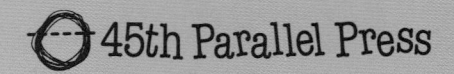

Published in the United States of America by Cherry Lake Publishing
Ann Arbor, Michigan
www.cherrylakepublishing.com

Reading Adviser: Marla Conn MS, Ed., Literacy specialist, Read-Ability, Inc.
Book Designer: Felicia Macheske

Photo Credits: © Dragon Images/Shutterstock.com, cover, 1; © Mammut Vision/Shutterstock.com, 3; © antoniodiaz/Shutterstock.com, 5; © Jason Stitt/Shutterstock.com, 7, 30; © untitled/Shutterstock.com, 9; © Alina555/iStock.com, 11; © Africa Studio/Shutterstock.com, 12; Phonlamai Photo/Shutterstock.com, 14; © Kozlik/Shutterstock.com, 15, 22, 31; © bowdenimages/iStock.com, 17; © MANDY GODBEHEAR/Shutterstock.com, 18; © Rawpixel.com/Shutterstock.com, 19, 25; © Monkey Business Images/Shutterstock.com, 20; © INSAGO/Shutterstock.com, 21; © RichLegg/iStock.com, 23; © Hurst Photo/Shutterstock.com, 27;© Olena Zaskochenko/Shutterstock.com, 28; © Odua Images/Shutterstock.com, 29

Graphic Elements Throughout: © pashabo/Shutterstock.com; © axako/Shutterstock.com; © IreneArt/Shutterstock.com; © Katya Bogina/Shutterstock.com; © Belausava Volha/Shutterstock.com; © Nik Merkulov/Shutterstock.com; © Ya Tshey/Shutterstock.com; © kubais/Shutterstock.com; © Sasha Nazim/Shutterstock.com; © Infomages/Shutterstock.com; © Ursa Major/Shutterstock.com; © topform/Shutterstock.com; © Art'nLera/Shutterstock.com; © Mari Ya/Shutterstock.com; © primiaou/Shutterstock.com

Copyright © 2018 by Cherry Lake Publishing
All rights reserved. No part of this book may be reproduced or utilized in any form or by any means without written permission from the publisher.

45th Parallel Press is an imprint of Cherry Lake Publishing.

Library of Congress Cataloging-in-Publication Data has been filed and is available at catalog.loc.gov

Cherry Lake Publishing would like to acknowledge the work of The Partnership for 21st Century Skills. Please visit *www.p21.org* for more information.

Printed in the United States of America
Corporate Graphics

ABOUT THE AUTHOR

Dr. Virginia Loh-Hagan is an author, university professor, former classroom teacher, and curriculum designer. She does improv games to practice public speaking. She lives in San Diego with her very tall husband and very naughty dogs. To learn more about her, visit www.virginialoh.com.

TABLE OF CONTENTS

Chapter One
What Does It Mean to Host an Improv Show?............ **4**

Chapter Two
What Do You Need to Host an Improv Show?............ **8**

Chapter Three
How Do You Set Up an Improv Show?................. **16**

Chapter Four
How Do You Run an Improv Show?.................. **24**

D.I.Y. Example................................... **30**

Glossary....................................... **32**

Index... **32**

Learn More..................................... **32**

CHAPTER ONE

WHAT DOES IT MEAN TO HOST AN IMPROV SHOW?

Do you like playing games? Do you like acting? Do you like being on stage? Then, hosting an **improv** show is the right project for you!

Improv is short for **improvisation**. This means making things up. Improv shows are a form of live theater. They're unique. No two shows are alike. Actors do improv on stage. They act in the moment. They don't plan. There aren't any **scripts**.

Scripts are prepared outlines. Actors make up the plot. They make up the characters. They make up the **dialogue**. Dialogue is what people say.

Talk to improv actors. Learn from them.

KNOW THE LINGO

Accepting: letting others help you move forward with the scene

Advancing: moving the scene forward

Breaking the routine: interrupting the action with another action in order to advance the scene

Callback: bringing back an idea from earlier in the scene

Gagging: making a joke that doesn't flow with the scene

Plateau: a period in which a scene is not advancing

Setup: explaining the scene to the audience before acting

Shelving: acknowledging an offer but not doing anything with it

Stepping out: breaking the acting by commenting

Talking heads: when actors do more talking than moving

Waffling: failing to make decisions

Walk-on: entering a scene, making an offer, and then exiting

Wimping: accepting an offer but not acting on it

Improv **troupes** are groups of actors. They practice together. They perform together. They do shows together. They do contests. They compete with other troupes. They travel together.

They take ideas from **audiences**. Audiences are viewers. They go to shows. They watch. They participate. They're a part of the show. They help create the story.

Host an improv show whenever you want! They're popular all year. Hosting these shows will give you more practice. You need to practice in front of audiences. You'll build your improv skills. You'll gain more confidence. You'll meet new people. The best part is you'll have fun.

Watch sketch comedy shows on TV.

CHAPTER TWO

WHAT DO YOU NEED TO HOST AN IMPROV SHOW?

Gain skills. Take improv classes. Get more comfortable on stage.

- Sign up for your level. There are different levels.
- Look for classes in your city. The most popular cities for improv are Chicago, Los Angeles, and New York City. But classes are all over.
- Go to classes often. Participate in everything.
- Practice as much as you can. Get better over time.

Go to live improv shows. Get ideas.

- Study performers.
- See what works well on stage. See what doesn't work.
- See how the audience responds.

Go to theaters. Some offer free classes.

Build community.

➡ Get people to know you.

➡ Support your friends as they perform.

➡ Invite them to your show.

Work on different types of improv. Decide what type of show you want to host.

➡ **Practice comedy. This is the most popular type. Comedy is funny. Its goal is to make people laugh.**

➡ **Practice drama. Drama is more serious. It makes people feel emotions.**

➡ **Practice short-form. These are short scenes. Audiences start the scenes. They give ideas. Short-form is also called theater games.**

➡ **Practice long-form. These are when short scenes are connected. The short scenes all have the same story. They have the same characters. They have the same themes. They can be plays.**

Combine types of improv shows.

Get a place.

- Find a space that has a stage area. This is for actors to move around.
- Find a space that has an area for people to sit and watch.
- Choose to be indoors or outdoors.
- Consider houses. Consider schools. Consider theaters. Use their big rooms. Move furniture around.

Get improv actors. You need people to perform.

- Host **auditions**. These are when people interview for a role.
- Have actors perform. See if they'll do well on stage. Test them out before the show.

Get a timer to time scenes.

TRY THIS!

Try this improv game. Create a scene with 26 lines of dialogue.

You'll need: people, bag, scene ideas

Steps

1. Pick a scene out of the bag. All lines must build this scene.
2. Group A stands in a circle. Group B waits.
3. The starting person says the first line. The first line starts with "A."
4. Move clockwise.
5. The second person replies. This person says the next line. This line needs to start with a "B."
6. Keep going until you get to "Z."
7. Group B replaces Group A members as they mess up. Players mess up by hesitating. They mess up by using the wrong letter. They mess up by not moving the scene along.
8. Play again. This time, Group B stands in a circle.

Get audience members. You need people to watch the show.

➡ **Ask friends and family.** Get them to attend.

➡ **Promote the event.** Get people to come.

Get an **emcee**. This is the host. This person makes announcements. This person introduces the event. This person moves the show along. This person closes the event. This person thanks everyone for coming.

➡ **Get someone who is comfortable speaking in public.**

➡ **Get someone who is funny. Get someone who has a lot of energy.**

➡ **Get someone who has a loud, clear voice.**

Get food and drinks.

➡ **Keep actors healthy. They talk a lot. Make sure you have water.**

➡ **Provide snacks and drinks for the audience. Consider charging small fees. This is a way to make some money.**

Audition the emcee.

CHAPTER THREE

HOW DO YOU SET UP AN IMPROV SHOW?

Set rules for the actors. Rules guide each **beat**. Beats are units of a scene.

- **Create the ask-for.** This is the question asked of the audience that starts the scene.

- **Listen to offers.** Offers are moves that advance the scene.

- **Agree.** Say yes and add something. Don't deny ideas. Go with the flow.

- **Don't block other people's ideas.** Blocking is stealing jokes. It's changing topics. It's rejecting others' ideas.

➡ Stay in character. Don't break the scene.

➡ Don't ask questions. Too many questions make others do too much work.

➡ Say whatever comes to your mind. Be silly. Have fun!

➡ Balance between give and take. Work as a team.

Give everyone a chance to shine.

Advice from the Field
ESE OSAGHAE

Ese Osaghae is from Chicago. He's an improv performer. He started in high school. He was part of the Second City Teen Improv Troupe. He is a student at John Carroll University. The university is in Ohio. Osaghae formed the Improvisation Club. He's the club president. The club members get together. They perform improv games. They do this on stage. They plan shows. They perform on campus. They compete in contests. They use the *Saturday Night Live* format. Osaghae advises having fun. He said, "The point of this whole thing is to have fun and genuinely laugh. We want everyone to come to the meeting and be relieved of stress."

Get actors used to each other.

Play improv games. This is like a **rehearsal**. Rehearsals are practice sessions. This builds teamwork. Improv is **collaborative**. It requires people to create something as a group. It gets people to build ideas off of each other.

- Look up games on the Internet.
- Read books about improv. They have game ideas.
- Get game ideas from classes.
- Hire an improv expert. This person can lead games for you.
- Keep the games short. Spend 2 to 10 minutes for each game.
- Move on to a new game before people get bored.
- Play games twice. This lets people improve.
- Record. Watch later. Discuss how you can improve.

Look at other programs. Get ideas.

Create a program. This is a little book. It gives details about the show.

- Include the show's date.
- Include the show's time.
- Include the show's place.
- Include photos of the actors.
- Include information about the actors. Include their names. Include their acting experiences.
- Include the events of the show.

Promote your show.

- Create a Web site.
- Use social media. Post videos of rehearsals.
- Make a **flyer**. This is information on a page. Give to everyone.

Set rules for the audience.

➡ **Tell people they're part of the show. People help move scenes along. They laugh. They cry. They react. They encourage actors.**

➡ **Tell people to give ideas. Their ideas inspire the show. They keep the show fresh. They keep the show from being planned. Actors will ask the audience for ideas. They'll ask for their thoughts.**

➡ **Tell people to open their minds. People need to imagine. Improv actors can't use real props. Props are objects. Instead, they do space work. This means they pretend. They pretend to have objects. They make motions. So, the audience has to believe.**

Explain what improv is to your audience.

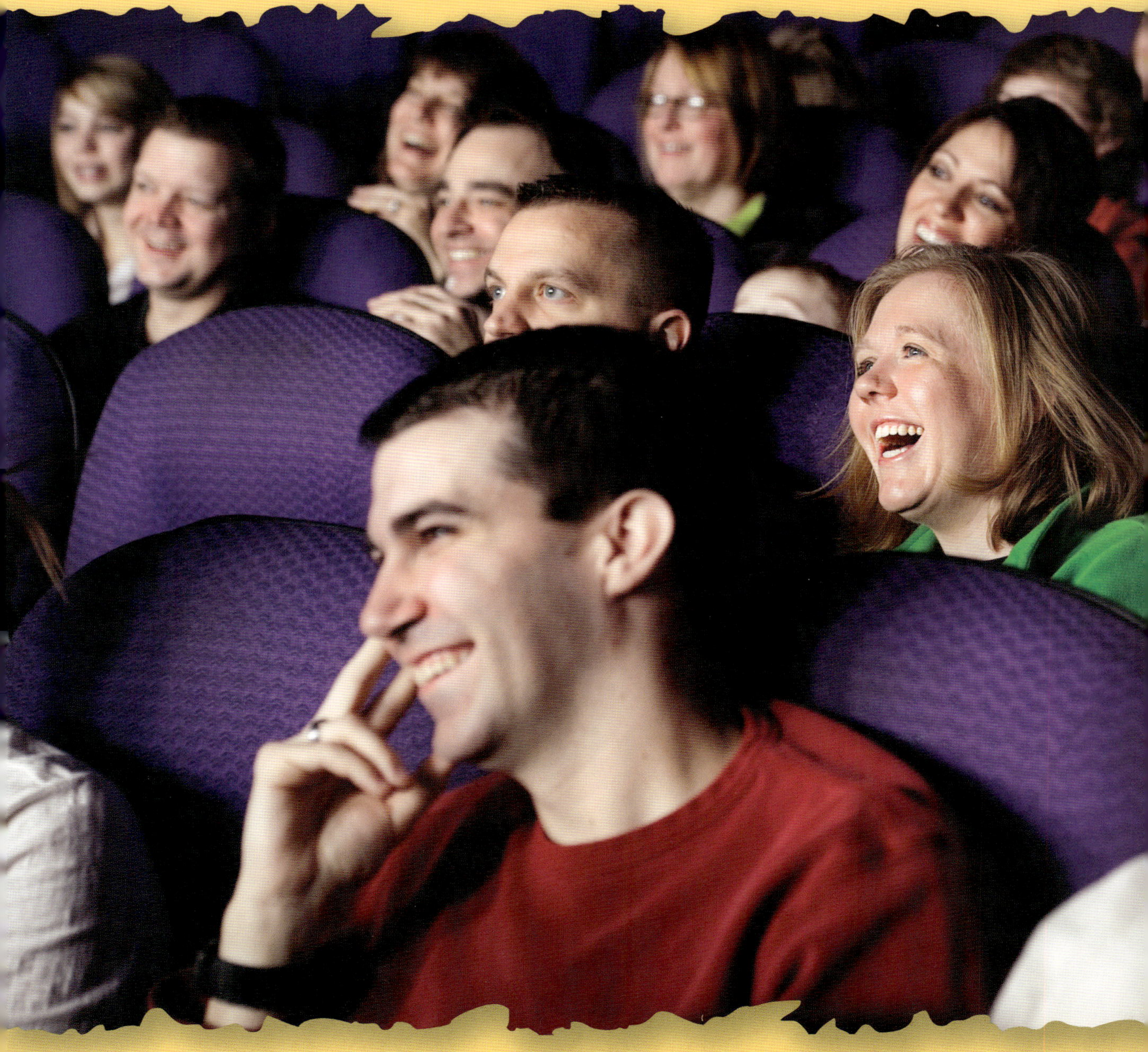

CHAPTER FOUR

HOW DO YOU RUN AN IMPROV SHOW?

You've got actors. You've got an audience. You've got a stage. Now, you're ready for your improv show!

Have the emcee introduce the show.

- Welcome everyone. Give out programs.
- Introduce the actors.
- Share the rules.
- Start with a **warm-up**. This is a practice activity. It gets people ready. Play an easy improv game. Choose a silly one. Make people laugh. Make them comfortable.

Structure your show. This is an example. Start with an opening.

➡ **Ask the audience for an idea. This sets the theme.**

➡ **Give the actors time to think about it.**

➡ **Have the actors perform.**

➡ **Act for 5 minutes.**

Create your own improv structure.

QUICK TIPS

- Stick with what you know. Don't make up crazy characters. Don't make up crazy plots.

- Listen to your teammates. React to them.

- Remember there is no right or wrong in improv. Work through your mistakes. Have fun.

- Show up. Don't miss any events.

- Take notes. Keep a diary. Write down what you learned. Record what happens to you.

- Shower. Be clean. You'll be working closely with your teammates.

- Live life. Get interesting experiences. Take chances. Use these stories for your improv.

- Focus on the scene. Don't focus on your role.

- Use an improv structure. Here's an example: long-form, about 40 minutes long, and has three scenes. This is called "the Harold."

Act out the first scene.

Play a game.

➡ **Let actors have fun.**

➡ **Ask audience for ideas.**

Act out the second scene.

➡ **Base scene on opening.**

Play another game.

Act out the third scene.

➡ **Build on second scene. End scene.**

Play final game. This is the **warm-down**. This is to wind down.

Have the emcee introduce each scene.

Have the emcee close the show.

- Thank the actors.
- Thank the audience for coming.
- Tell people about future events.
- Sell **merchandise**. These are things you can sell or give away. Examples are shirts, hats, and posters.

Host a **post-show** discussion. This happens after the show.

- Meet with actors.
- Talk about what went well.
- Talk about what didn't go well.

Clean your area.

Get comfortable on stage. Consider hosting contests. Do this in the future.

- **Invite several improv troupes. Have them compete against each other.**
- **Have each group act.**
- **Have the audience be judges.**
- **Have the emcee announce awards.**
- **Have fun!**

D.I.Y. EXAMPLE!

STEPS	EXAMPLES
Name of improv troupe	The Stage Queens: All-Girl Improv
Date	Friday night
Place	Private room at a restaurant
Plan show	This show is a short-form comedy. It'll feature improv games. Each game or scene will be 8 minutes long. ♦ Welcome and introductions ♦ Improv game #1: Bucket ♦ Improv game #2: Walk Out ♦ Improv game #3: Audience choice—let audience members pick an improv game out of a hat ♦ Closing ♦ Post-show discussion

STEPS	EXAMPLES
Improv games	Bucket: • Have audience write simple sentences. Do this on slips of paper. • Put these slips into a bucket. • Ask an audience member to set the scene. • Act out the scene. • Pull out a slip every couple of minutes. Use this in dialogue. Walk Out: • Get three actors. • Give each actor a word. Use common words. • Start a scene with two actors. Ask audience for ideas. • Act out the scene. When actors hear their words, they leave the scene. When they hear their words again, they return to the scene.

GLOSSARY

ask-for (ASK-for) question asked of the audience that starts a scene

audiences (AW-dee-uhns-iz) people who go to see a show or movie, viewers

auditions (aw-DISH-uhnz) interviews where people act to get a role

beat (BEET) unit of a scene

block (BLAHK) to reject other people ideas, to steal jokes, to change topics

collaborative (kuh-LAB-uh-ruh-tiv) a group effort that requires working together

dialogue (DYE-uh-lawg) lines that people say when they're talking to each other

emcee (em-SEE) the host of a show

flyer (FLYE-ur) information on paper used for promotion

improv (IM-prov) short for improvisation

improvisation (im-prah-vuh-ZAY-shuhn) making things up, acting without a script

long-form (LAWNG-form) connected short scenes like a play

merchandise (MUR-chuhn-dise) things that can be sold or given away for promotion

post-show (pohst-SHOH) after the show

props (PRAHPS) objects used in a play or movie

rehearsal (rih-HURS-uhl) practice session

scripts (SKRIPTS) prepared outlines

short-form (SHORT-form) short disconnected scenes, theater games

space work (SPAYS WURK) pretending to have props

troupes (TROOPS) groups, acting companies

warm-down (WORM-doun) practice activity that winds people down after the main event

warm-up (WORM-uhp) practice activity that prepares people for the main event

INDEX

actors, 7, 12, 16, 28
audiences, 7, 14, 22
beats, 16
emcee, 14, 24, 28
games, 10, 13, 19, 27

improv show
  D.I.Y. example, 30–31
  how to set one up, 16–23
  promoting, 21
  quick tips, 26
  running one, 24–29
  types of, 10

improv show (cont.)
  what is needed, 8–15
  what it is, 4–7
  where to have one, 12
lingo, 6
program, 21

LEARN MORE

BOOKS

Bedore, Bob. *101 Improv Games for Children and Adults.* Alameda, CA: Hunter House, 2004.

Belli, Mary Lou, and Dinah Lenney. *Acting for Young Actors: The Ultimate Teen Guide.* New York: Back Stage Books, 2006.

Zimmerman, Suzi. *More Theatre Games for Young Performers: Improvisations and Exercises for Developing Acting Skills.* Colorado Springs, CO: Meriwether Publishing, 2004.

WEB SITES

Improv Encyclopedia: http://improvencyclopedia.org

Improv Games: www.improvgames.com/category/game/

Second City Teen Troupe: www.secondcity.com/classes/hollywood/teen-troupe/